MW00834114

THE EARLY
POLO GROUNDS

This vintage poster advertises the 1887 baseball schedule for the New York Giants. This is when the team played at the original Polo Grounds, located at 110th Street between Fifth Avenue and Sixth (now Lenox) Avenue, directly across 110th Street from the northeast corner of Central Park. The game of polo was in fact played at this site, which is how the stadium got its name—a name that would remain when the new stadium was built a few years later.

On the front cover: Please see page 13. (Courtesy Library of Congress, Prints and Photographs Division.)

On the back cover: Giants take the field before the start of the 1912 World Series. (Courtesy Library of Congress, Prints and Photographs Division.)

Cover background: Game 4 of the 1912 World Series is seen here. (Courtesy Library of Congress, Prints and Photographs Division.)

THE EARLY POLO GROUNDS

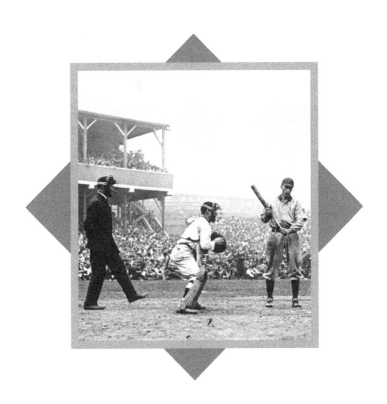

Chris Epting
Foreword by Arnold Hano

ARCADIA
PUBLISHING

Published by Arcadia Publishing
Charleston SC, Chicago IL, Portsmouth NH, San Francisco CA

Library of Congress Catalog Card Number: 2008929988

For all general information contact Arcadia Publishing at:
Telephone 843-853-2070
Fax 843-853-0044
E-mail sales@arcadiapublishing.com
For customer service and orders:
Toll-Free 1-888-313-2665

Visit us on the Internet at www.arcadiapublishing.com

This book is dedicated with love and affection to my cousin,

friend, and fellow Polo Grounds fan, David McAleer.

CONTENTS

ACKNOWLEDGMENTS

This book would not have been possible without the photographs of George Grantham Bain (1865–1944). Bain was a New York photographer who founded the Bain News Service in 1898. His news photograph service had special emphasis on life in New York City, and many of his wonderful images reside today at the Library of Congress Prints and Photographs Division, where many of the photographs in this book were culled from. Special thanks also to the Pictorial History Committee of the Society for American Baseball Research (SABR) and its members Bill Carle, Joe Dittmar, Bill Hickman, Bill Loughman, Joe Murphy, Tom Shieber, and Mark Stang for reviewing the collection and providing dates and player identifications.

I'd also like to acknowledge several important books that have helped me immensely over the years (and given me much joy): *Ballparks of North America*, by Michael Benson; *Land of the Giants*, by Stew Thornley; *Baseball Memories 1900–1909*, by Marc Okkonen; *Green Cathedrals*, by Philip Lowry; *A Day in the Bleachers*, by Arnold Hano; and *Lost Ballparks* and *The Glory of Their Times*, both by Lawrence Ritter.

As far as all of the additional research I have done, I take full responsibility for any errors—every effort has been made to ensure accuracy. Thanks as well to my mom; my wife, Jean; son, Charlie; and daughter, Claire for their patience (as always) through the process. And to the great writer Arnold Hano for writing a truly magical foreword for this book—thank you so much, Mr. Hano. I am grateful for your generosity and will always be indebted to you.

FOREWORD

Back in 1957, my agent Sterling Lord persuaded *Sports Illustrated* to assign me to cover the last ball game the New York Giants would host in the Polo Grounds. The following season the team would be the San Francisco Giants, and they would be playing their home games at Seals Stadium, while Candlestick Park was being built.

I flew from California to New York, bought a seat in the center field bleachers for 75¢ and watched the young Pittsburgh Pirates thrash my Giants, 9-1.

When the game mercifully ended, the fans erupted onto the playing field, tearing up swaths of dirt and grass, tearing up the bases, tearing away the pitcher's slab, uprooting home plate. Far-sighted fans had come armed with screwdrivers, and presto, seats were removed. The fans eventually left, laden with their booty.

I left, clutching my rain check, and laden only with memory.

I had seen my first major-league baseball games in the Polo Grounds, beginning in 1926, when I was four years old. It was easy then. My grandfather was a New York City cop with season passes to both the Polo Grounds and Yankee Stadium. The Polo Grounds was closer; my family lived a long downhill block from the Giants park. I went to games the way other kids went to camp.

And I remember.

I remember John McGraw, standing arms akimbo in the third base coaching box, where he would direct traffic when his Giants were batting. McGraw was never a man to linger in the dugout shadows, though of course that was where he had to be stationed when the Giants were in the field. At bat, there would be Mugsy, constantly in motion, flashing signs, stopping runners at third, pinwheeling them home when an outfielder paused for a split second in getting to a base hit. I watched him so often I began to imitate his stance, my hands at my hips, and kids in the neighborhood starting to call me Mugsy.

I remember Bill Terry, so graceful at first base, so powerful at the plate, driving a long fly ball over a center fielder's head, the ball rolling to the Eddie Grant plaque at the end of the runway between the two sections of the bleachers, Terry tearing around the bases for an inside-the-park home run.

I saw Mel Ott raise his front leg and heard the fans chortling, "Hey, Melvin, I wanna hear you bark." To which Ott's response would be a line drive into the upper deck in right field.

I remember Travis Jackson at shortstop, going into the hole and then gunning a rifle shot throw across to Terry, to nip a fleet runner. And second baseman Hughie Critz, whom we called the Groundskeeper because he'd go out every inning to his position and carefully pick up ever pebble or hard clod of earth, and stuff them into his back pocket, all to prevent a ground ball from taking a bad hop past him. And oh so fat Shanty Hogan, the Giants catcher, truly a giant, perhaps nearing 300 pounds, slower than any player in the league with the possible exception of

Ernie Lombardi against whom Travis Jackson would station himself 30 feet into left field, where he could collar Lombardi's hot smashes and easily throw him out. That's how they built catchers back then, 80 years ago, slow as horse-drawn ice wagons. And I remember "King" Carl Hubbell as he tormented batters with his elusive screwball.

Some of my memories were not so positive. One day I saw the combative Giants shortstop Billy Jurges confront umpire George Magerkurth, on a call Jurges violently objected to, the two men standing jaw to jaw, raging invective at each other. A faint spray of saliva emitted from Magerkurth's mouth; Jurges stepped back and uncorked his own oyster of spittle, right in the umpire's face. Magerkurth slugged Jurges, who slugged him back, and the two men rolled on the infield grass, clawing at each other until they were pried apart. Jurges, of course, was tossed out of the game and suspended for a spell, his place at shortstop taken over by mild-mannered prematurely gray utility infielder, Lou Chiozza. The very next day, Chiozza ran out to short left field, chasing a pop fly, while in rushed Joe Moore, from his left field post. The result was a noisy collision, which sent Chiozza to the hospital, marking the first and only time one player's spittle had broken another player's leg.

And I remember the wondrous Willie Mays, playing the game with the youthful glee of a kid, beginning in 1951 and continuing until the Giants left in 1957, the fans in the bleachers around me chanting, "Go, Horace, Go, Stay, Willie, Stay!" Horace was the Giants' owner, Horace Stoneham, committing an act of betrayal in taking his Giants 3,000 miles away.

Nor was my attendance at the Polo Grounds limited to baseball games. I sat in the lower left field stands to watch the championship professional football game between the undefeated Chicago Bears led by Bronc Nagurski and the New York Giants. Because the field was so icy slick—the temperature dipped to four degrees above zero that Sunday afternoon—the Giants' owner Wellington Mara had a minion at halftime break into Manhattan College's gymnasium and steal the school's basketball sneakers. Clad in the sneakers and suddenly able to keep from sliding all over the joint, the Giants turned a 13-3 deficit into a 30-13 victory. All this despite an advisory to his teammates from a former Chicago linebacker named George Halas, "Step on their toes! Step on their toes!"

Over those years I saw boxing matches, I saw Negro League ball games, I saw football games, both college level and professional. I got to know the Polo Grounds about as well as I knew my backyard. The glorious green of the outfield grass, the painted foul lines, the flags unfurled above the stadium—all this was my milieu. After a ball game, my brother and I would race onto the field, run the bases, stand at the pitcher's mound and imagine we were Hubbell facing the dreaded Hornsby or—shudders running down our spines—even Babe Ruth!

People today will ask me, as Californians are often asked, "Where did you grow up?"

And I answer only somewhat facetiously, "I grew up in the Polo Grounds."

—Arnold Hano, author of *A Day in the Bleachers*

INTRODUCTION

I cannot explain what it is that fascinates me about the bathtub-shaped ballyard known as the Polo Grounds. I never went there (it was torn down in 1964, I was born in 1961). But I was born in New York City, so it's possible that I may have passed it in a car as a young child. Still I have no personal history there, so I'm left thinking it was the photographs I saw of the Polo Grounds when I was young, in all of my baseball books. It looked so inviting, intimate, and cozy, with so many peculiar angles and vantage points. As a Little Leaguer, I dreamed of what it must have been like to both play and wander there. In the upper deck, in the bleachers near the subway trains and, most of all, from up on Coogan's Bluff, where fans gathered atop the rocky hill to watch for free (although only a sliver of the field was visible). Built in 1891, the Polo Grounds played host to some iconic baseball moments, including Willie Mays's famous catch in the 1954 World Series and Bobby Thomson's "shot heard 'round the world." But the era before those moments, back when the New York Giants, Yankees, and the football Giants shared the park, holds history all its own. Christy Mathewson, John McGraw, Jim Thorpe, and many others live on today in dramatic black-and-white images. The beginning of the 20th century through the 1920s is a rarely seen chapter in Polo Grounds history, and that's what inspired me to present it in this collection.

Throughout the text in the book, the park's history through this important era will reveal itself. The chapters are broken down into an order that I found logical—I hope it makes sense to you. I've tried to include as much information as I can about specific players who are pictured at the Polo Grounds; after all, a park's history is only as rich as the people who played and performed there.

I also included a chapter in this book about some of the other ballparks in the area, and a chapter documenting a trip I made with my son back to the original site of the Polo Grounds. It's my hope that someday, someone will write a book (or series of books) which document, through photographs, the Polo Grounds era(s) that followed this one.

Lastly, a poem by Rolfe Humphries about the Polo Grounds appeared in *The New Yorker*, August 22, 1942. It is titled *Polo Grounds*, and this is an excerpt from it—little did Humphries know how well his words would reflect the images contained herein:

> Time is of the essence. The rhythms break,
> More varied and subtle than any kind of dance;
> Movement speeds up or lags.
> The ball goes out in sharp and angular drives, or long slow arcs,
> Comes in again controlled and under aim;
> The players wheel or spurt, race, stoop, slide, halt,

Shift imperceptibly to new positions,
Watching the signs according to the batter,
The score, the inning. Time is of the essence.
Time is of the essence. Remember Terry?
Remember Stonewall Jackson, Lindstrom, Frisch,
When they were good? Remember Long George Kelly?
Remember John McGraw and Benny Kauff?
Remember Bridwell, Tenney, Merkle, Youngs,
Chief Meyers, Big Jeff Tesreau, Shufflin' Phil?
Remember Mathewson, Ames, and Donlin,
Buck Ewing, Rusie, Smiling Mickey Welch?
Remember a left-handed catcher named Jack Humphries,
Who sometimes played the outfield, in '83?
Time is of the essence. The shadow moves. From the plate to the box, from the box to second base,
From second to the outfield, to the bleachers.
Time is of the essence. The crowd and players
are the same age always, but the man in the crowd
is older every season. Come on, play ball!

THE EARLY

POLO GROUNDS

This spectacular view of the Polo Grounds, shot from beyond right field, was taken during the 1913 World Series. In this particular series, the Philadelphia Athletics defeated the Giants, four games to one. It is just two years after a fire gutted almost the entire grandstand.

From atop Coogan's Bluff (named for James J. Coogan, local land owner and Manhattan's first borough president) behind the ballpark, fans could see part of the field for free. Many would gather up here on days when big games were being played, where they could also enjoy a view across the East River, where after 1923, Yankee Stadium would be plainly visible. This view is from 1909, and a year later, a wooden approach from the speedway on Coogan's Bluff would be built that would allow spectators to enter the second level of the grandstand. In this shot, recent expansion has resulted in the park extending around the entire field, so carriages could no longer park up on the running track just outside center field.

An infamous baserunning blunder by New York Giant Fred Merkle during a game against the Chicago Cubs at the Polo Grounds on September 23, 1908, resulted in the October 8, 1908, replay of the game. This image shows a dispute at first base between the two clubs during this pivotal game.

THE EARLY POLO GROUNDS

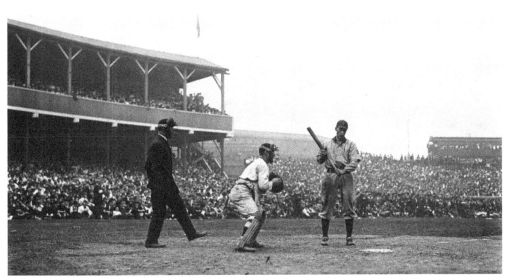

Roger Bresnahan is catching for the New York Giants in a game versus Pittsburgh on September 18, 1908, at the Polo Grounds. Even though Bresnahan was taunted by other players, he experimented with head and thigh padding, which had been introduced by some college teams. This led to the widespread use of more protection for catchers in the early 20th century (and Bresnahan is wearing some of the revolutionary gear in this photograph). The iconic Y beams supporting the upper and lower grandstand are clearly visible. (Courtesy Library of Congress, Prints and Photographs Division.)

On Friday, April 14, 1911, a fire of unknown origin swept through the horseshoe of the grandstand portion, consuming the wood and leaving only the steel uprights in place. The gaps between some sections of the stands saved a good portion of the outfield seating, as well as the clubhouse, from destruction. The Giants temporarily rented Hilltop Park from the Yankees while they began to rebuild the Polo Grounds double-decked grandstand with concrete and steel. Here players from New York and Philadelphia tour the charred remains of the ballpark the very day it burned.

The original date on this wonderful panorama of the Polo Grounds is October 13, 1910. The season ended just two days before that and the Giants did not play in the postseason that year, so most likely this is from the last day of the season (or so), October 11, versus the Philadelphia Phillies.

This is the Polo Grounds on Saturday, August 13, 1904. The New York Giants were playing Cincinnati and the attendance was 24,625.

This photograph shows a World Series game at the Polo Grounds in October 1905, between the American League Philadelphia Athletics and the National League New York Giants.

This image from underneath the first base–side roof overhang was taken in 1910 during a game between Boston and New York. The wooden Y beams would be lost in a fire the next year.

In 1908, the Chicago Cubs and Giants were tied in the standings at the end of the season, so they replayed a tied game from two weeks earlier. On this last day of the season, the Cubs won, 4-2, thus claiming the pennant. This shot from that October 8 captures some of the raucous fans in the outfield stands.

This shot of fans leaving the Polo Grounds was also taken at that tumultuous final game, October 8, 1908. Note how virtually every fan is wearing a shirt, tie, and hat.

This image of the outfield wall at the Polo Grounds was taken in 1911, and several members of the Philadelphia Phillies can be seen in the photograph.

That is New York Giant Fred Merkle at bat, Giant Red Murray walking in background, and an unidentified catcher at the Polo Grounds during the 1911 World Series, which featured the Giants versus the Cincinnati Reds. What is not explained on the original photograph notes are why, mysteriously, the stands are so empty.

The right field bleachers are packed on Tuesday, October 8, 1912, for Game 1 of the 1912 World Series. The Giants would lose this game, 4-3, and lose the series, four games to three (there were actually eight games played in the series—Game 2 ended in a 6-6 tie and was called on account of darkness).

This photograph illustrates how ornate the decorative friezes were at the "new" Polo Grounds, which rose from the ashes of the 1911 fire. The upper deck facade featured bas-relief allegorical treatments, while the roof facade featured National League team insignias (a detail that can be found in Stew Thornley's excellent book *Land of the Giants*).

There are many interesting details in this shot from Game 1 of the 1912 World Series, including the right field foul pole and rope that divides fair/foul territory, the decorative eagles atop the stadium roof, the scoreboard near the lower center of the shot, and of course, the close play at second.

Fans sit in the left field bleachers on Tuesday, October 8, 1912, Game 1 of the World Series.

The Boston Red Sox take batting practice before Game 1 of the 1912 World Series at the Polo Grounds.

Telegraphers are shown here behind home plate at the Polo Grounds during the 1912 World Series. This early version of the press box was designed for the electrical telegraph operators who would report on events live from the scene.

The New York Giants are arriving for batting practice before Game 1 of the 1912 World Series. Legendary manager John McGraw can be seen at right, in white. The players' clubhouse building can be seen at left center; it is from where the Giants just emerged (and the building itself a remnant from old Manhattan Field, moved over in 1904).

This is Game 4 of the 1912 World Series, held on October 11. The Red Sox beat the Giants 3-1 this game and would go on to win the series four games to three.

New York Yankee president Frank Farrell is seated in his box seats at the Polo Grounds, in this photograph, taken sometime between 1903 and 1911 (he is resting his head in his hand). The Yankees sublet the Polo Grounds from the Giants during 1913–1922, after their lease on Hilltop Park expired. After the 1922 season, the Yankees built Yankee Stadium directly across the Harlem River from the Polo Grounds, a situation that spurred the Giants to expand their park to reach a seating capacity comparable to the stadium, to stay competitive. Note the distinctive wooden Y beams, which would be destroyed in the Polo Grounds fire of 1911.

Early warm-ups take place before a game on May 7, 1913, between the New York Giants and the Cincinnati Reds. The Giants would win later in the day, 6-4. Note the wall advertisements for Fatima Cigarettes, "Bull" Durham Smoking Tobacco, and the Uneeda Biscuit billboard, which sits atop the players' clubhouse beyond right field.

This is Hal "Prince Hal" Chase, legendary Chicago White Sox first baseman, at the Polo Grounds, around 1915. The subway can be seen running just outside the outfield wall, as can many of the advertisements, including one for the *Saturday Evening Post*.

This weather-damaged photograph was taken October 7, 1913, at the first game of the World Series. The Philadelphia Athletics defeated the New York Giants 6-4 this day and would go on to win the series four games to one. This image was taken from the right field grandstand.

Game 1 of the 1913 World Series is pictured from the right field stands, with the Giants at bat (hall of famer Eddie Collins of the A's can be seen here at second base).

The right field bleachers are shown on Thursday, October 9, 1913, Game 3 of the World Series. Philadelphia defeated New York 8-2 to take a two games to one lead in the series. In this shot, the Giants' winning banners from previous years can be seen on the flagpole near the center of the photograph.

Philadelphia Athletic Eddie Collins lays down a bunt in Game 3 of the 1913 World Series. Note the "keyhole" path from the pitcher's mound to home plate.

Batting practice has just ended, and the press is clearing the field on October 7, 1913, just before Game 1 of the World Series.

Photographers are pictured with their box cameras on field before Game 1 of the 1913 World Series at the Polo Grounds.

Here is another shot from Game 3 of the 1913 World Series.

This splendid shot of the Polo Grounds shows the Philadelphia Athletics running off the field after defeating the New York Giants 12-5 in Game 3 of the 1913 World Series. They are headed toward the clubhouse seen beyond the right field wall.

Fans were allowed to leave the Polo Grounds by walking on the field, and this image was taken at the end of Game 3 in the 1913 World Series.

THE EARLY POLO GROUNDS

Note the box seats running out toward left field in this other image taken after Game 3 of the 1913 World Series.

This image from Game 3 of the 1913 World Series was taken from the players' clubhouse beyond right field. Note the picket fence separating standing room from the bleachers.

Telegraphers are pictured at the Polo Grounds during the 1913 World Series.

Players warm up at the Polo Grounds in this *c.* 1912 photograph. Note the photographers to the left and brass band to the right.

THE EARLY POLO GROUNDS

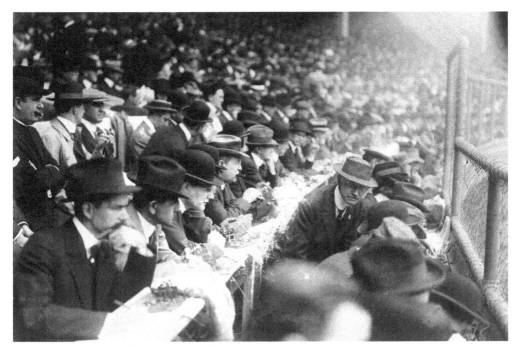

Reporters are pictured at the 1913 World Series.

The left field bleachers are jam-packed at the 1913 World Series.

The Polo Grounds as seen from under the stands down the first-base line during the 1913 World Series.

It is April 15, 1916, at the Polo Grounds. Frank Gilhooley of the New York Yankees slides in to third base in this wonderful image shot from the third base box seats.

In Game 3 of the 1917 World Series, shown here, the Giants beat the White Sox 2-0 but went on to lose the series four games to two. This incredible angle, shot from the left field roof of the Polo Grounds clearly shows the elevated subway that brought fans to the game. As well, the rope tied to the foul pole indicating fair/foul territory is visible.

A marching band leads the Giants out on field during the pregame festivities of opening day at the Polo Grounds, April 16, 1918.

This is another angle from opening day in 1918 as the parade around the field continues.

New York Yankee Elmer Miller scores in Game 1 of the 1921 World Series on October 5. The Yankees won this game 3-0 but went on to lose the series five games to three (back then the series was won in five games instead of four like today). Since both teams shared the Polo Grounds, all games in the 1921 series were played here.

THE EARLY POLO GROUNDS

In the fifth inning of Game 1 in the 1921 World Series, Yankee third baseman Mike McNally led off with a double and was moved over to third with a bunt. He then stole home, as seen in this photograph, to put the Yankees in front 2-0.

The bleachers are packed during the 1921 World Series between the New York Giants and the New York Yankees.

This is a different angle of the bleachers during the 1921 World Series between the New York Giants and the New York Yankees.

This is the Polo Grounds on April 20, 1923. Yankee Stadium is now located just across the Harlem River and opened officially just two days before this photograph was taken. The soon-to-be familiar center field clubhouse building is under construction at the Polo Grounds, and the Eddie Grant memorial can be seen in deep center field.

THE EARLY POLO GROUNDS

In this 1923 image of the Polo Grounds, major construction is underway. The frieze has been removed from the roof facade, and the ballpark is beginning to assume the design it will maintain until it is demolished in 1964.

The New York Giants and the Boston Braves prepare to kick off the 1923 season at the Polo Grounds.

National League Baseball
Park, New York

This postcard image of the Polo Grounds, around 1915, features an image of manager John McGraw.

National League Base Ball Park, New York, N.Y.

This is an earlier postcard image, which depicts the Polo Grounds in 1905.

THE EARLY POLO GROUNDS

2

THE GIANTS AT
THE POLO GROUNDS

The New York Giants pose for a 1911 team photograph. An advertisement for Odol oral care products has been plastered across roof facade. Within just a week or so, the infamous Polo Grounds fire would all but destroy the stadium, and its look would be changed forever.

Mike Donlin (nicknamed "Turkey Mike" because of his gait while walking) became an almost instant idol to Giants fans just after he arrived in 1904. A great hitter, he bested .300 ten times in 12 major-league seasons. After 1908, Donlin left baseball for a fling at a vaudeville and movie career (by then he was married to actress Mabel Hite). After three successful years treading the boards, Donlin did return to the game in 1911 to his old team and manager, John McGraw. This image is from the day he came back to the Giants, June 28, 1911, and it is also the date the Polo Grounds opened after the fire several months earlier. The new structure stretched in roughly the same semicircle as before from the left field corner around home plate to the right field corner and was also extended into deep right-center field. The surviving bleachers were retained for the most part, with gaps remaining between the bleachers and the new fireproof construction.

The great New York Giants pitcher Christy Mathewson warms up at the Polo Grounds before the 1911 World Series. The Athletics would beat the Giants in the series, four games to two.

Christy Mathewson, or "Matty" as he was called, takes batting practice before the 1911 World Series. Manager McGraw had the Giants don their black broadcloth uniforms as a means of intimidating the Athletics, but it did not seem to work as it had in years past.

New York Giants shortstop Art Fletcher warms up before the 1911 World Series. After his career as a player, Fletcher began a 19-year tenure (1927–1945) as a coach for the Yankees. On a somewhat tragic note, he served as the acting manager of the Yankees for the last 11 games of the 1929 season when manager Miller Huggins was fatally stricken with blood poisoning. He won 6 of those 11 games, to compile a career major-league-managing record of 237-383 (.382).

New York Highlander manager Harry Wolverton is pictured at left with Giants skipper John McGraw in 1912. Based on research, this image comes from a charity game held to raise money for the survivors of the *Titanic*, which sank on April 14 (three days before it is believed this photograph was taken). The Giants beat the Highlanders 11–2. In another year, the Highlanders would be known exclusively as the Yankees.

Two legends at the Polo Grounds, John McGraw and Johnny Evers, are pictured here in 1912. Note that the Giants wore pinstripes before the Yankees, who would soon introduce their now iconic design.

The New York Giants pictured at the Polo Grounds on opening day, April 10, 1913. From left to right are Fred Snodgrass, Tillie Shafer, George Burns, Larry Doyle, Red Murray, Fred Merkle, Buck Herzog, and Chief Meyers.

Game faces are on display as the New York Giants are arriving for batting practice before Game 1 of the 1912 World Series. Legendary manager John McGraw can be seen at right, in white. The players' clubhouse building can be seen at right center; it is from where the Giants just emerged.

New York Giant John Tortes "Chief" Meyers takes batting practice at the Polo Grounds in 1910. (Note the original Y-beam grandstand supports.) Meyers was a talented catcher and in his career played for the New York Giants, Boston Braves, and Brooklyn Robins from 1909 to 1917. He played on the early Giants teams under manager John McGraw and was the primary catcher for hall of famer Christy Mathewson. Meyers, a Cahuilla Indian from California, was educated at Dartmouth College.

What a difference a year makes. It is 1912, and the Polo Grounds is in the process of being rebuilt after the devastating fire of 1911. The grandstand is taking shape, but the new decorative facade has yet to be placed on the overhang.

New York Giants manager John McGraw hits some batting practice at the Polo Grounds in 1918. Nicknamed "Little Napoleon" and "Mugsy," McGraw remains one of the toughest, most effective managers (and players) in history.

Christy Mathewson prepares to hit some fielding practice at the Polo Grounds in 1911, just a day or two before the fire that devastated the ballpark.

This 1913 image features an out-of-uniform Christy Mathewson on the left shaking hands with someone identified as "W. Courtenay."

This is Giants pitcher Charles Bunn "Bunny" Hearn at the Polo Grounds in 1913. Following the 1913 season, Hearn was a member of John McGraw's world touring team. At a game in London, Hearn explained the various grips pitchers used on the ball to King George V. Later in life, he would often brag that he taught the King of England how to throw a curve.

Chief Meyers takes some batting practice at the Polo Grounds in 1912.

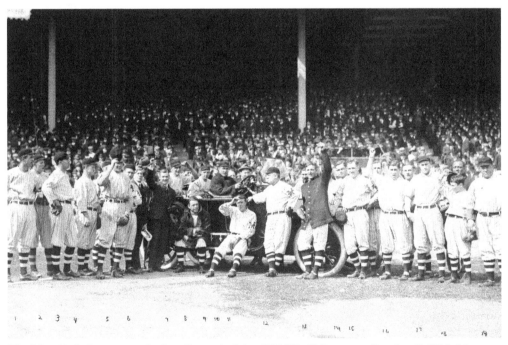

The New York Giants pose before Game 1 of the 1912 World Series on October 8, 1912. Manager McGraw is near the center of the photograph, Mathewson just to the right with his arm raised.

That's Tillie Shafer on the left and hall of fame Giants pitcher Rube Marquard on the right in 1912 at the Polo Grounds. In 1908, when the New York Giants purchased Marquard's contract for the unprecedented price of $11,000, many eyebrows were raised. Two years later, when he was still in search of his 10th major-league victory, the press derided him as the "$11,000 Lemon." When skipper John McGraw was about to give up on him, Marquard went on a tear, winning a total of 73 games from 1911 to 1913, including a 19-game winning streak in 1912.

A 1912 team photograph shows the Giants at the Polo Grounds.

Doc Crandall is on the left and Fred Snodgrass is on the right, both of them New York Giants, at the Polo Grounds 1912. Snodgrass played in three consecutive World Series for the Giants from 1911 to 1913. Unfortunately the Giants lost all of them, and he is remembered for committing an error on a routine fly ball in the 10th inning of the deciding game, which allowed the Boston Red Sox to win the 1912 series. The play was forever known as "Snodgrass's Muff." Despite the infamy of the "muff," the play only resulted in the ultimately tying run being put onto second base. It did not cause any runs to score.

These are New York Giants recruits posing at the Polo Grounds in 1913. Front and center is famed Olympian (and sometime baseball player) Jim Thorpe. In 1913, Thorpe started his six-season Major League Baseball career with the New York Giants, under manager John McGraw, just one year after decimating the world's best in the decathlon and pentathlon in Stockholm at the 1912 Olympics.

Jim Thorpe is seen as a New York Giant at the Polo Grounds in 1913. This year, Thorpe was stripped of his two gold medals after the Amateur Athletic Union discovered that he played for a minor-league baseball team from 1909–1910. Plenty of amateur athletes played professional ball in those days, but did so under assumed names.

Here is another shot of Thorpe at the Polo Grounds, posing in his new pinstripes.

This is a simple, magnificent portrait of Thorpe.

Seen here is a 1913 New York Giants team portrait at the Polo Grounds. Thorpe is in the back row, fifth from the left. Christy Mathewson and John McGraw are front and center.

This is a New York Giants team portrait taken to open the season on April 10, 1913.

Here is a wonderful group portrait at the Polo Grounds from May 1913. From left to right are Josh Devore (New York), Tillie Shafer (New York), Larry Doyle (New York), Dick Egan (Cincinnati), Grover Hartley (New York), and Beals Becker (Cincinnati). Some great details are here, in the fencing, the chairs, and the onlookers.

John McGraw hits batting practice in 1914 at the Polo Grounds.

Another team portrait from August 1913 is shown above. As usual, Christy Mathewson and John McGraw are right up front. Can you spot Chief Bender and Jim Thorpe? (Bender is fifth from left, first row. Thorpe, fifth from right, second row.)

New York Giants Christy Mathewson (left) and Jeff Tesreau (right) are seen here in 1914 at the Polo Grounds. From 1912 to 1917, Tesreau was a starting pitcher with the Giants. In 1918, he had an argument with John McGraw and quit the Giants in the middle of the season. In 1919, Tesreau refused to play for the Giants. McGraw refused to trade or release Tesreau, and so Tesreau took a position as baseball coach for Dartmouth College, a job he held until his death on September 24, 1946.

A 1913 New York Giants team photograph outtake is shown above.

During his career, Hans Lobert was known as one of the fastest players in the game. He even once raced a racehorse around the bases before a game. He finished his career with the New York Giants at the Polo Grounds and is seen here in 1917, the last year he played professional baseball (although he would go on to manage and work as a scout until his death).

New York Giants players help raise the flag in honor of opening day in 1923 at the Polo Grounds. Judge Kennesaw Mountain Landis is visible to the left, standing next to the cop, hat in one hand and walking stick in the other. Construction taking place in the far right stand upper deck is visible as well.

John J. "Red" Murray of the Giants practices his slide into third in this 1913 image, which provides a nice view of the players' clubhouse beyond right field. From 1909–1912, Murray ranked third in the National League in total RBIs, trailing only Honus Wagner and Sherry Magee. He and Wagner tied for the most home runs in the majors from 1907 through 1909 (21).

Giants pitcher Ferdie Schupp warms up in 1913. The southpaw helped the Giants win the 1913 and 1917 National League pennant and led the National League in won-loss percentage (.750) and hits allowed per nine innings pitched (6.68) in 1917. The Polo Grounds redesign is all but complete and will remain like this until the 1930s.

3

THE VISITORS
(AND THE YANKEES)
AT THE POLO GROUNDS

Yankee slugger Babe Ruth is seen here at the Polo Grounds in 1921 during the World Series. The Giants defeated the Yankees five games to three, and since the teams shared the park, all eight games were played at the Polo Grounds.

Cy Falkenberg of the Cleveland Indians is pictured at the Polo Grounds in 1913. Falkenberg attended the University of Illinois, becoming one of the few university-educated ballplayers of the time. He debuted with the Pittsburgh Pirates on April 21, 1903, but struggled his first year in the majors, losing five of six decisions. He spent 1904 back in the minor leagues. He returned to the majors in 1905, this time with the Washington Senators, but he did not achieve his greatest success until 1913 with the Cleveland Naps.

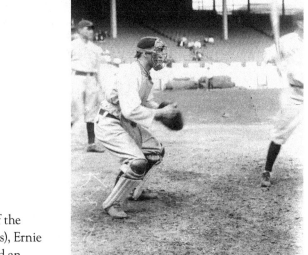

This 1913 image shows Nap Lajoie of the Cleveland Indians at left (out of focus), Ernie Krueger is catching for Cleveland and an unknown Giants batter is at the plate.

Cincinnati manager Joe Tinker at the Polo Grounds in 1913 is seen here. Tinker is perhaps best known as the shortstop in the Tinker to Evers to Chance double-play combination immortalized in the poem "Baseball's Sad Lexicon" by New York newspaper columnist Franklin Pierce Adams. Yet on September 14, 1905, he and Evers ended up in a fistfight on the field because Evers took a cab and left his teammates behind in the hotel lobby. They did not speak to one another for 33 years until they were both asked to help broadcast the 1938 World Series (Cubs versus Yankees) and tearfully reunited.

It is Babe of the Yankees—not Ruth, but Babe Borton, racing around first in 1913 on a day when the stands are almost completely empty. A subway train can be seen off in the distance by the *Saturday Evening Post* sign.

This 1912 image shows Pfeifer Fullenweider, a New York Giants pitching prospect from Columbia, South Carolina, in the South Atlantic League. He may not have made a name for himself in baseball, but his name lives on as one of the most unique of any ballplayer.

This image stars Edward Victor Cicotte, a pitcher for the Chicago White Sox, in 1914. Nicknamed "Knuckles," Cicotte was one of eight players permanently ineligible for professional baseball for his alleged participation in the Black Sox scandal in the 1919 World Series, in which the favored White Sox lost to the Cincinnati Reds in eight games.

First baseman Jack Fournier of the Chicago White Sox is at the Polo Grounds in 1913. Fournier hit 136 career home runs in 14 seasons while averaging .313 with a .393 on-base percentage. He also racked up three straight seasons with 20-plus home runs, 20-plus doubles, a .400 or higher on-base percentage, a .330-plus batting average, and 90-plus runs.

This 1913 batting practice image features the White Sox players Walt Kuhn behind the plate catching and Larry Chappell at bat.

Babe Ruth of the New York Yankees warms up along the first-base line at the Polo Grounds in 1921. Babe Ruth's first home run as a Yankee came on May 1, 1920, over the Polo Grounds roof in right field. It was said to have landed in Manhattan Field, which at that point was just was a vacant lot. Soon after, it was paved over, and became a parking lot for the Polo Grounds.

Babe Ruth poses with some young fans before the start of the 1921 World Series at the Polo Grounds.

Babe Ruth is seen here warming up at first base sometime during the 1921 season, when the Yankees still shared the Polo Grounds with the Giants. (The Yankees would move out in 1923 when Yankee Stadium was opened just across the Harlem River.)

Seen here are, from left to right, Eddie Murphy, John "Shano" Collins, "Shoeless Joe" Jackson, Happy Felsch, and Nemo Leibold. The White Sox are at the Polo Grounds for Game 3 of the 1917 World Series, a series the White Sox won, four games to two.

Yankee pitcher Carl Mays is seen here at the Polo Grounds in 1922. One of the better right-handed hurlers from 1916 to 1926, he is also remembered for throwing the pitch that struck Ray Chapman in the head on August 20, 1920, at the Polo Grounds. This made Chapman only the second major leaguer in history to die as a direct result of an on-field incident (he died the next day at a New York City hospital—see below).

This is Ray Chapman of the Cleveland Indians, at the Polo Grounds in 1919, a year before he was fatally wounded there. He is the second of only two Major League Baseball players to have died as a result of an injury received in a game (the first was Mike "Doc" Powers in 1909). His death led Major League Baseball to establish a rule requiring umpires to replace the ball whenever it became dirty. His death was also one of the examples used to emphasize the need for wearing batting helmets (although the rule was not adopted until over 30 years later). His death was partially the reason Major League Baseball banned the spitball after the season.

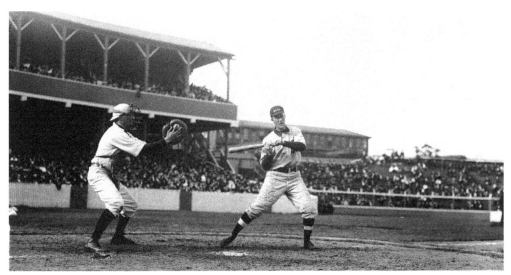

The caption on this photograph reads, "Stock Brokers Ball Game (New York - Boston), N.G. Greenaway (New York) at bat, W. Clark (Boston) catching." It is dated May 22, 1908. Beyond that, there is not any other concrete information known regarding this photograph.

Seen here is Jimmy Archer of the Chicago Cubs at the Polo Grounds on July 21, 1910. Archer was an Irish-born catcher who spent nearly his entire career with four National League teams, primarily the Chicago Cubs, for whom he played from 1909 to 1917. Born in Dublin, he also played for the Pittsburgh Pirates in 1904, the American League's Detroit Tigers in 1907, and the Pirates, Brooklyn Robins, and Cincinnati Reds in 1918. As a catcher, he could remain squatting and still throw out runners attempting to steal second base due to his unique arm strength, which became his trademark. It was acquired from the healing of burns that shortened his muscles after an industrial accident in which Archer fell into a vat of boiling sap at the age of 19.

Chicago Cub great Frank Chance is here at the Polo Grounds in 1912. As a first baseman and manager, Chance led the Chicago Cubs to four National League championships in the span of five years (1906–1910) and earned the nickname the "Peerless Leader." Of course, he was also part of the infield trio remembered in "Baseball's Sad Lexicon," a poem by newspaper columnist Franklin Pierce Adams first published in 1910 and also known as "Tinker to Evers to Chance." Note the on-field potted plant.

The great Red Sox pitcher Howard Ellsworth "Smoky Joe" Wood is here at the Polo Grounds during the 1912 World Series. After joining the Red Sox in 1908, Wood had his breakthrough season in 1911 in which he won 23 games, compiled an ERA of 2.02, threw a no-hitter against the St. Louis Browns, and struck out 15 batters in a single game. Wood once struck out 23 batters in an exhibition game. He earned the nickname "Smoky Joe" because of his blazing fastball. Wood once said, "I threw so hard I thought my arm would fly right off my body."

Billy Kelly was 24 years old when he broke into the big leagues on May 2, 1910, with the St. Louis Cardinals. By 1912, he played for the Pittsburgh Pirates, and that is the year this shot was taken at the Polo Grounds. His career lasted only four seasons in the majors. Note the advertisement for Adams Pepsin Chewing Gum in the outfield.

Alex McCarthy was a middle infielder who came to the Pittsburgh Pirates in 1910 from the University of Notre Dame and spent most of his career with the Pirates. A teammate of Honus Wagner, he was either a double play partner for Wagner or a backup to him for several years. This image of him at the Polo Grounds was taken in 1912.

This is Claude Hendrix of the Pittsburgh Pirates at the Polo Grounds in 1912. While pitching for the Chicago Whales of the Federal League, Hendrix tossed a no-hitter against Pittsburgh in May 1915. And there is some infamy. As a Chicago Cub, Hendrix agreed to throw a game in August 1920 and was subsequently banned from baseball. Interestingly Hendrix did not actually take the mound. The Chicago Cubs, suspecting wrongdoing, substituted Grover Cleveland Alexander for Hendrix at the last minute. Still he paid the price. Following his involuntary departure from baseball, Hendrix owned and operated a café in Allentown, Pennsylvania, for many years until his death in 1944.

Bill Killefer, nicknamed "Reindeer Bill," both caught and managed in the majors. He had a 12-year career for the St. Louis Browns, Philadelphia Phillies, and Chicago Cubs. He played for the 1915 Phillies team that lost to the Boston Red Sox in the World Series, and after the 1917 season, he was traded to the Cubs with Grover Cleveland Alexander for two players and $55,000 in cash. In 1918, he played in another World Series, losing again to the Red Sox. He retired from playing at age 33 in 1921, becoming the manager of the Cubs shortly after. This image at the Polo Grounds was taken in 1912.

George W. Chalmers was born in Aberdeen, Scotland, and pitched in the majors from 1910 to 1916. He played for the Philadelphia Phillies and is seen here at the Polo Grounds in 1912. Note how thick the grass is and the planter on field behind Chalmers.

The great Frank "Homerun" Baker is seen here practicing at the Polo Grounds in 1916. Baker, who led the American League in home runs in 1911, earned the nickname "Homerun" during the 1911 World Series in which he hit a go-ahead home run off Rube Marquard in Game 2 and a ninth-inning game-tying home run off Christy Mathewson in Game 3. Baker, who would be elected to the Professional Baseball Hall of Fame in 1955, called the Polo Grounds home for five season as a Yankee, and as can be seen, he is wearing the famous pinstripes in this image.

Dode Paskert played outfield in the major leagues from 1907 to 1921. He would play for the Philadelphia Phillies, Cincinnati Reds, and Chicago Cubs. In this 1912 image, he is a member of the Phillies. Note the players' clubhouse to the right of the image.

John P. Henry of the Washington Senators bats at the Polo Grounds around 1915. Henry played in the majors for nine years, from 1910 to 1918.

Bob Groom was a pitcher in two Midwest minor leagues and the Pacific Coast League from 1904 to 1908 and then in the major leagues from 1909 to 1918. He pitched for the Washington Senators, St. Louis Terriers (Federal League), St. Louis Browns, and Cleveland Indians. He is seen here in 1915 at the Polo Grounds as a Washington Senator.

This is Yankee pitcher Ray Caldwell at the Polo Grounds in 1913. Known for throwing the spitball, he was one of the 17 pitchers allowed to continue throwing the pitch after it was banned in 1920. Caldwell was notorious during his playing career for his addiction to alcohol, and he possessed a self-destructive streak that many believed kept him from reaching his potential.

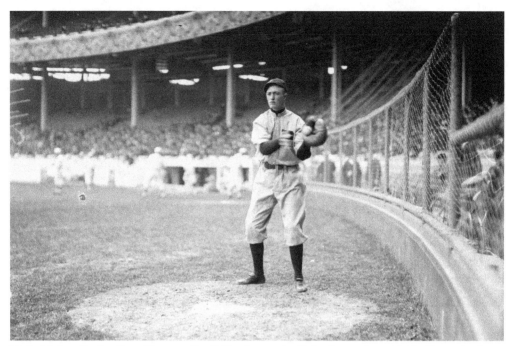

Philadelphia Phillie Dan "Dapper Dan" Howley at the Polo Grounds in 1913. He pitched just one season in the majors but went on to manage for several seasons after that. This image provides good detail of the fence that protected patrons behind the backstop.

Albert "Cozy" Dolan of the Philadelphia Phillies is seen at the Polo Grounds in 1913. He played for six teams during his 13-year career. Note the VIP seats to the left of the dugout behind Dolan.

Phillies pitcher Eppa Rixey was the National League's leader in career victories for a left-hander until Warren Spahn. Throughout his long career, Rixey charmed teammates and fans with his dry wit and big Southern drawl. His nonsensical nickname "Jeptha" seemed to capture his blue-blood roots and amiable personality. Rixey was inducted into the Professional Baseball Hall of Fame in 1963. This image of him at the Polo Grounds was taken in 1913.

This 1914 image shows Phillies pitcher George Chalmers at the Polo Grounds in 1914.

In this 1913 image, Hans Lobert is playing for the Phillies (he would end his career at the Polo Grounds as a Giant in just a few seasons).

Eddie Grant was the only major leaguer killed in World War I. Grant entered the majors with the Cleveland Indians at the very end of the 1905 season, played for the Philadelphia Phillies, the Cincinnati Reds (who he is playing for in this 1913 image), and finally, the New York Giants. Nicknamed "Harvard Eddie," Grant graduated from Harvard and practiced law after his retirement from baseball. Grant was one of the first men to enlist when the United States entered World War I in April 1917, and he served as captain of the 77th Infantry Division. During the fierce battle of the Meuse-Argonne Offensive, all of Grant's superior officers were killed or wounded, and he took command of his troops on a four-day search for the "Lost Battalion." During the search, an exploding shell killed Grant on October 5, 1918. Shortly after his death, a bronze plaque was installed in deep center field at the Polo Grounds to honor Grant. When the Giants left New York after the 1957 season, the plaque mysteriously disappeared.

John P. Henry of the Washington Senators is seen at the Polo Grounds in 1914. Note the rough condition of the grass and the padded wall behind the practice plate.

Pitcher Jimmy Lavender of the Chicago Cubs is at the Polo Grounds in 1912. Lavender was primarily a spitballer in his career and used it to win 16 games as a 28-year-old rookie in 1912. He would not equal that success again, winning only 10 or 11 games in each of his last four seasons in Chicago. Lavender threw a no-hitter on August 31, 1915, against the New York Giants and also threw a one-hitter against them on June 14, 1916, allowing only an infield single to Benny Kauff. In this image, a Bull Durham advertisement can be seen on the outfield wall.

Cleveland's Lee Dashner is at the Polo Grounds in July 1913. Dashner played for one season for the Cleveland Naps; in fact, he pitched in just one game (on August 4, 1913).

Kid Gleason, manager of the Chicago White Sox, hits some practice grounders in 1918 at the Polo Grounds. Gleason is best known as the betrayed manager of the 1919 Chicago White Sox, the team made infamous by the Black Sox scandal, in which Gleason's players conspired to intentionally lose the World Series. The Black Sox scandal resulted in lifetime bans from baseball for eight White Sox players. Gleason, however, had no knowledge of the conspiracy. Although he felt betrayed and disappointed by his 1919 team, he continued to manage the White Sox until 1923.

From left to right are Jimmy Lavender, Ward Miller, Charlie Smith, and Tommy Leach of the Chicago Cub, posing at the Polo Grounds in 1913.

The legendary Johnny Evers at the Polo Grounds is seen here in 1913. Evers is best known to modern-day fans as the pivot man in the Tinker to Evers to Chance double-play combination, which inspired the classic baseball poem, "Baseball's Sad Lexicon," by New York newspaper columnist Franklin Pierce Adams. He was also the player who alerted the umpires to Fred Merkle's baserunning error in the 1908 pennant race, costing the Giants the pennant.

Seen here is Cincinnati pitcher Armando Marsans at the Polo Grounds in 1913. Marsans and teammate Rafael Almeida are regarded by some historians as the first athletes born in Cuba to play in the major leagues. (This distinction is disputed because Cuban-born Steve Bellán played from 1871 to 1873 in the National Association, which is regarded by some historians as a major league, but is not recognized as a major league by Major League Baseball.) Marsans and Almeida debuted together with the Reds on July 4, 1911.

St. Louis pitcher Doc Crandall is at the Polo Grounds in 1913. Over the course of his career from 1908 to 1918, Crandall would play for the Boston Braves, St. Louis Browns, St. Louis Terriers, and New York Giants. Crandall was also the first major-league pitcher to be used consistently as a reliever.

Yankee third baseman Fritz Maisel is seen at the Polo Grounds in 1913. Because of his speed on the base paths, his fans knew Fritz as "Catonsville Flash" or just "Flash." In 1914, he led the American League with 74 stolen bases and was only caught stealing 17 times that year, an 81 percent success rate.

Here is Pittsburgh catcher Bob Coleman at the Polo Grounds in 1913. In addition to playing, Coleman also was one of the most successful managers in the history of minor-league baseball, his career extending (with interruptions caused by major-league service) from 1919 through 1957.

Cleveland catcher Ernie Krueger at the Polo Grounds in 1913 is shown above. In addition to playing for the Naps, Kreuger also helped the Giants win the 1917 National League pennant and the Robins win the 1920 National League pennant.

Chicago Cub Frank Chance is at the plate and Cubbie Pat Moran is behind the plate in this 1909 image from the Polo Grounds.

Cy Falkenberg of the Cleveland Indians is pictured at the Polo Grounds in 1913. He was known for throwing the "emery ball," a baseball that had been scuffed with a piece of emery board hidden in the heel of his glove. Although this practice is currently against the rules of baseball, it was legal at the time. By scuffing the ball, the ball moves in a less predictable manner, making it harder to hit, giving him a 23-10 record in 1913.

This is the legendary Honus Wagner at the Polo Grounds in 1913. In 1936, the Professional Baseball Hall of Fame inducted Wagner as one of the first five members, receiving the second-highest vote total behind Ty Cobb and tied with Babe Ruth. Although Cobb is frequently cited as the greatest player of the dead-ball era, some contemporaries regarded Wagner as the better all-around player, and most baseball historians consider Wagner to be the greatest shortstop ever. Cobb himself called Wagner "maybe the greatest star ever to take the diamond."

St. Louis pitcher Walter Leverenz in a 1913 image at the Polo Grounds is seen above. The team clubhouse is clearly visible just to the left of Leverenz.

John "Shano" Collins of the Chicago White Sox takes batting practice in 1920 at the Polo Grounds. He played first base for the White Sox, but he was quickly moved to right field, where he developed a reputation for having one of the strongest throwing arms in baseball. He won a World Series with the White Sox in 1917, delivering the game-winning hit in the pennant-clinching game. He was traded to the Red Sox in 1921, where he finished his career. In 1930, he was named manager of the Red Sox, but he only won a total of 73 games in parts of two seasons. ("Shano" was a nickname given to him while on the White Sox, which is a play on the Gaelic equivalent of his name, Sean.)

Here is Philadelphia pitcher Grover Cleveland "Old Pete" Alexander at the Polo Grounds in 1917. One of the greatest pitchers in history for the Philadelphia Phillies, Chicago Cubs, and St. Louis Cardinals, he was elected to the Professional Baseball Hall of Fame in 1938.

Another image of Grover Cleveland Alexander at the Polo Grounds in 1917 is seen here. Alexander was born in Elba, Nebraska. He signed his first professional contract at age 20 in 1907 for $50 per month. He had a good first season, but it was marred by a beaning that probably contributed to later bouts with epilepsy. This incident set his career back, but he had recovered by 1910, became a star pitcher again, and was sold to the Philadelphia Phillies for $750.

This is Boston Braves outfielder George "Hickory" Jackson at the Polo Grounds in 1913.

In the 1917 World Series, the Chicago White Sox beat the New York Giants four games to two. In this image, the White Sox take the field for Game 3, held on October 10. The series was played against the backdrop of World War I, which dominated the American newspapers that year and next. A marching band is seated off to the left, and the youngster at the center of the shot is most likely a White Sox batboy.

THE FANS AND
PERSONALITIES AT
THE POLO GROUNDS

Mayor William Jay Gaynor arrives at opening of the 1910 baseball season at the Polo Grounds. Gaynor served as mayor of the city of New York from 1910 to 1913, as well as stints as a New York Supreme Court justice from 1893 to 1909. Gaynor is also the only New York City mayor to suffer an assassination attempt.

The caption of this photograph reads: "Stock Brokers Ball Game (New York - Boston), Manager New York team J.F. Carlisle, also C.R. Runyon, and Ira Richardson." The date is May 22, 1908. While it has been hard to uncover any more information about it, the visual details are fascinating. The patchy ground, wood plank fence, ornate walking sticks held by the archly posing men—it is a very interesting photograph.

Fans, some seated on the fringe of the outfield grass, are packed in for the final game in 1908, October 8, the legendary deciding game of the season versus the Chicago Cubs.

Ty Cobb pays a visit to the Polo Grounds during the 1911 World Series and is seen here chatting with New York Giants pitching ace Christy Mathewson.

Mayor William Jay Gaynor (second from left) arrives at the opening of the 1913 baseball season at the Polo Grounds. A band can be seen playing to the far right.

Here Giants fans leave the park on the Eighth Avenue elevated subway after watching the Giants drop Game 1 of the World Series to the Philadelphia Athletics on October 7, 1913.

Justice of the Supreme Court Edward McCall presents a silver basket of flowers to New York Giants manager John McGraw at the Polo Grounds before Game 1 of the 1913 World Series on October 7, 1913.

John Brush Hempstead, son of the New York Giants president Harry Hempstead and grandson of the late John T. Brush (former president of the New York Giants), throws out the first pitch of Game 1 of the 1913 World Series at the Polo Grounds.

That is famed boxer "Gentleman Jim" Corbett (center, wearing the derby) and Blossom Seeley (wife of Rube Marquard) to Corbett's left at Game 1 of the 1913 World Series at the Polo Grounds. Corbett's brother Joe Corbett pitched in the majors for a number of teams including the Washington Senators and the St. Louis Cardinals.

Here are Red Sox fans at the Polo Grounds on October 8, 1912, Game 1 of the 1912 World Series (the Red Sox would eventually win the series four games to three). Note the new steel girders holding up the grandstand, as well as the Boston Delegation sign hanging on a post to the right.

Mayor John Purroy Mitchel is seen here at the Polo Grounds throwing out the first pitch of the 1915 season. Called the "Boy Mayor of New York," Mitchel was New York City's youngest mayor in history, elected to office when he was just 34. He was defeated when he tried for reelection and died less than six months after he left office, at age 38. He had been training to join the Army Air Corps in World War I and tragically fell 500 feet out of his biplane after forgetting to fasten his seat belt.

Here is Mayor Mitchel once more, a year after the previous shot, tossing out the first pitch to kick off the 1916 season at the Polo Grounds.

The date is April 11, 1917. That is Gen. Leonard Wood at the Polo Grounds shaking hands with an unidentified Yankee while Yankee manager "Wild Bill" Donovan looks on at right. Wood was an unsuccessful candidate for the Republican presidential nomination in the election of 1920. He won the New Hampshire primary that year but lost at the convention.

Here is Wood shaking Donovan's hand. Later in his career, Donovan was accused of having some knowledge of the attempt to throw the 1919 World Series but was vindicated by Commissioner Kenesaw Mountain Landis and sent an apology from his accuser, William Baker, president of the Philadelphia Phillies.

Gen. Leonard Wood (left) poses at the Polo Grounds with Maj. Gen. Halstead Dorey, who would go on to command the Pacific operations of the U.S. Army from 1934 to 1935. A graduate of the U.S. Military Academy in 1897, Dorey saw action in the Spanish-American War in the Philippines and in the subsequent Philippine Insurrection. He also took part in multiple campaigns during World War I.

Silent screen actress Alice Baldwin and producer Daniel Frohman enjoy a game from a front row at the Polo Grounds around 1916.

New York City police commissioner Richard Enright and his wife are seen here at the Polo Grounds in 1918.

This is Australian Archbishop Daniel Mannix of Melbourne, tossing out the first pitch in 1920 at the Polo Grounds.

Umpires and coaches meet before the start of the 1921 World Series between the Yankees and Giants.

Mrs. Chief Meyers (left) and Mrs. Larry Cheney (right) cheer their husbands on at the Polo Grounds in 1916.

THE FANS AND PERSONALITIES AT THE POLO GROUNDS

On Sunday, April 21, 1912, a week after the *Titanic* sank, the Giants and Yankees met at the Polo Grounds to play an unscheduled charity game to raise money for the survivors of the tragedy. Song-and-dance man George M. Cohan was on hand and is seen here rousing the crowd in support of the event.

Here is another shot of Cohan (in the checkered cap) at the *Titanic* game in 1912 at the Polo Grounds. At this time, teams were banned from charging admission to baseball games played on Sundays. To get around this, instead of selling tickets, the Giants required that fans purchase a program to attend the exhibition game.

A chorus girl is helping to raise money from the crowd at the *Titanic* charity game on April 21, 1912.

Another chorus girl at the *Titanic* game is seen here.

FOOTBALL AND
OTHER EVENTS AT
THE POLO GROUNDS

A lot of football was played here over the years, and not just by the New York Giants. Many college games were played here as well, including Carlisle versus Syracuse on October 6, 1909 (Carlisle won the game, 14-11). The Morris-Jumel Mansion (also known as the Roger and Mary Philipse Morris House), located on Coogan's Bluff, is visible to the upper right of the photograph. It is the oldest house in Manhattan. It served as a headquarters for both sides in the American Revolution and still stands today.

The Polo Grounds also hosted music performances over the years. Here, from left to right, the quartette of Giovanni Zenatello, Lucile Lawrence, Maria Gay, and Léon Rothier perform Verdi's *Requiem* at the Polo Grounds in 1916.

On April 3, 1909, a marathon with a race purse of more than $10,000 was held at the Polo Grounds. The field included Henri St. Yves, a waiter from France and marathon novice. St. Yves actually won the race by more than five minutes. The five-lap outdoor track built at the Polo Grounds was also used for other marathons that year at the stadium.

This photograph is captioned "Here Come the Players – Actors do stunts for crippled children. Polo Grounds, 7/17/08. Race for Prima Donnas won by Mabel Hite." Giants player Mike Donlin was married to Mabel Hite, a popular vaudeville and Broadway actress, pictured in this photograph.

This photograph is from the 1916 Army-Navy football game that was held at the Polo Grounds. Army won this contest, 15-7. The famed college rivalry was also played here 1913–1915, 1919–1921, 1923, 1925, and 1927.

This is another image from the Carlisle-Syracuse game on October 6, 1909. Famed athlete Jim Thorpe, who played baseball at the Polo Grounds as a New York Giant, was arguably the most famous student that Carlisle produced.

This image shows more action from the Carlisle-Syracuse game on October 6, 1909. Although the Polo Grounds had an odd shape for baseball, the elongated field seemed to be a very sensible design for a gridiron.

In this shot from the 1909 Carlisle-Syracuse game, many of the outfield wall advertisements are visible.

This is the Carlisle football team on October 6, 1909. The Carlisle Indian Industrial School, (1879–1918), was an Native American boarding school in Carlisle, Pennsylvania. It was founded in 1879 by Capt. Richard Henry Pratt at a disused barracks in Carlisle. The so-called "noble experiment" was a failed attempt to forcibly assimilate Native American children into the culture of the United States. The United States Army War College now occupies the site of the former school.

On November 15, 1913, Carlisle defeated Dartmouth by a score of 35-10 before a crowd of 10,000. This was two years after the Polo Grounds fire, and the newly designed friezes are visible at the top of the stadium.

On June 4, 1916, choral societies from New York and New Jersey took part in a large scale, open-air presentation of Verdi's *Requiem*. In this image, the instrumentalists can be seen sitting in the outfield bleachers at the Polo Grounds.

Here is another image from the Carlisle-Dartmouth game of November 15, 1913.

Cadets from West Point line the field at the 1916 Army-Navy game. The two buildings just to the left of the water tower still stand today.

Many classic fights were staged at the Polo Grounds, including one of the most famous of all time, Jack Dempsey versus Luis Firpo on September 14, 1923. A sold-out crowd of 82,000 people (with over 40,000 more being turned away at the gate) watched the champion, Dempsey, defend his title against the fierce challenger. This painting depicts a scene from the fight.

Edwin Franko Goldman (1878–1956) was a founder of the American Bandmasters Association and its first president. A composer, scholar, and prominent conductor, in 1911 he formed his own band, which in 1918 began a summer concert series, later know as the Guggenhiem Memorial Concert Series, in New York City. In 1918, he performed with his band at the Polo Grounds.

NEIGHBORING BALLPARKS

OF THE POLO GROUNDS

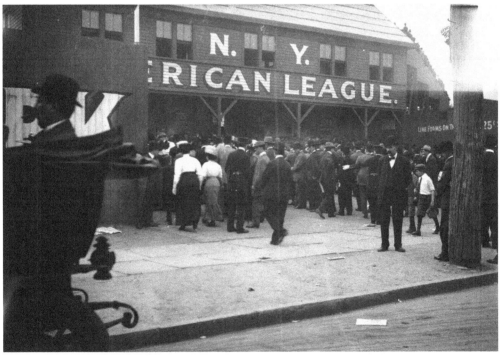

This is the entrance to Hilltop Park, around 1912, 10 blocks north of the Polo Grounds. It was the home of the New York American League major-league baseball team during 1903–1912 (the Highlanders, later called the New York Yankees). It was also the temporary home of the New York Giants during a two-month period in 1911 while the Polo Grounds was being rebuilt after the fire. As the signs read, grandstand seats are 75¢ and general admission tickets are just 50¢.

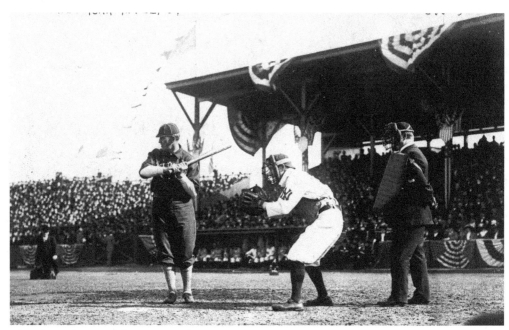

This shot taken at Hilltop on April 22, 1909, features Washington's Otis Clymer at bat and New Yorker Ron Kleinow behind the plate. The bunting hanging from the roof area is in honor of the fact that it is the home opener for the New Yorkers.

This image shows just how small, simple, and almost ramshackle Hilltop Park was. The single decks and wooden Y beams create about as basic as a major-league ballpark that existed back then. This image was taken on opening day, April 14, 1908, when the Philadelphia Athletics were visiting the New York Highlanders.

New York Highlander Curt Coleman warms up at Hilltop Park in 1912. Coleman was 25 years old when he broke into the big leagues on April 13, 1912, with the Highlanders, and so this is his rookie year. Note that the three buildings pictured to the left of Coleman still stand today, as pictured below.

In terms of the surrounding neighborhood, these three apartment buildings on West 168th Street, seen in so many of the old Hilltop Park photographs, are the only buildings in the immediate area that survive from back then. (See above.)

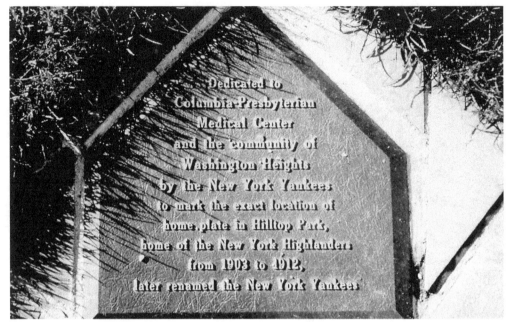

In 1993, through the efforts of the Society for American Baseball Research, a marker was placed to commemorate the original location of home plate at Hilltop Park. Today it is the site of the Columbia Presbyterian Medical Center.

The Brooklyn Tip-Tops, or "BrookFeds," of the short-lived Federal League were perhaps the only major-league team ever named for a loaf of bread. They acquired the ballpark property known as Washington Park in Brooklyn in 1914, then rebuilt the second Washington Park in steel and concrete. The old park took on a modern appearance; in fact, it was nearly a duplicate of the initial version of another Federal League park in Chicago that would become Wrigley Field. However, with the Dodgers in a new and somewhat more spacious steel-and-concrete home already, Ebbets Field, there was no long-term need for Washington Park, so it was abandoned for the final time after the Federal League ended its two-year run. This image shows the flag being raised on opening day on April 10, 1915. Other Federal League teams are listed on the scoreboard, along with the Dodgers and Yankees.

This image shows fans outside Washington Park in Brooklyn, at Third Avenue, looking east, around 1910. A sign advertises "field seats" for 25¢.

This image is from outside Brooklyn's Ebbets Field in 1920. The beloved park was located in the Flatbush section of Brooklyn and was the home of the Brooklyn Dodgers of the National League. Two different incarnations of a Brooklyn Dodgers football team also used Ebbets Field as their home stadium, as did the Brooklyn Tigers of the second American Football League. Ebbets Field was all but abandoned by the Dodgers after 1957, when the team moved to Los Angeles, and the ballpark was demolished in 1960. Today an apartment building stands in its place.

Pennsylvania governor John K. Tener throws out the first pitch at Ebbets Field in 1914. From 1885 to 1890, Tener had played professional baseball as both a pitcher and an outfielder for Cap Anson's Chicago White Stockings. From 1914 to 1918, Tener was president of the National League of Professional Baseball Clubs and in 1931 was elected as director of the Philadelphia National League Baseball Club.

Genevieve Ebbets, the youngest daughter of Charles Ebbets, throws the first ball at the opening of Ebbets Field on April 5, 1913.

This image captures Game 1 of the 1920 World Series between the Cleveland Indians and the Brooklyn Robins (called the Robins during this period in reference to their manager Wilbert Robinson). This image shows the left field corner at Ebbets Field. Beyond the wall, it can be seen how undeveloped the area still is.

Yankee Stadium, located just across from the Polo Grounds, is seen about two weeks before the official opening in April 1923. The stadium has since been replaced with a new model next door to this location.

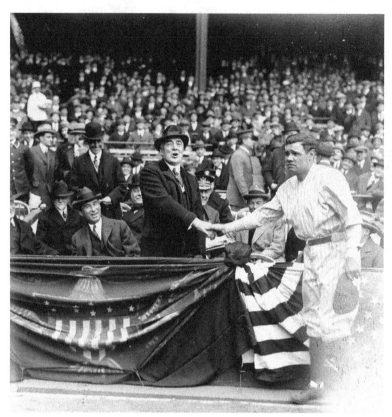

Yankee slugger Babe Ruth greets Pres. Warren Harding at the official opening of Yankee Stadium on April 18, 1923.

The ticket booths outside Yankee Stadium are seen here on opening day, 1923.

This image shows opening day fanfare at the new Yankee Stadium, 1923. The Polo Grounds is located just out of frame to the right, immediately across the Harlem River, less than a mile away.

Officials gather on field at the opening of Yankee Stadium. Note the batboy in the New York dugout.

Fans line up for World Series bleacher seats at Yankee Stadium in 1923. The Yankees would go on to beat their cross-river rivals, the New York Giants, in six games. The series of course alternated between the Polo Grounds and the new Yankee Stadium.

Originally the second Polo Grounds, Manhattan Field hosted baseball for one season after 1889, when the Giants were evicted from the original Polo Grounds in Manhattan. The Players League built a stadium called Brotherhood Park on the northern parcel of Coogan's Hollow for the 1890 season, but after one year, the league folded. In 1891, the Giants moved into Brotherhood Park and changed the name to the Polo Grounds (Polo Grounds III). Manhattan Field was converted for other sports such as football and track and field and still existed as a structure next door to the Polo Grounds for nearly 20 more years. The High Bridge, built between 1837 and 1848 and is still standing today, can be seen in the distance.

THE SITE OF THE
POLO GROUNDS TODAY

How compelling it must be to walk through a housing complex today, knowing the rich cultural history that took place right there, such as Christy Mathewson, John McGraw, Babe Ruth, and hundreds of other players, the millions of fans, and the memories so thick that the air still feels charged. It was right here, the Polo Grounds. Today at the former site, several Polo Grounds Towers signs can be found. Oddly the ballpark art on the signs looks nothing like the stadium itself. Completed in 1968, Polo Grounds Towers includes four buildings containing 1,616 apartment units. (Photograph by the author.)

This view is taken from the approximate site of the center field bleachers, looking toward first base. An elevated subway would have been located just behind where the photograph was taken. (Photograph by the author.)

This image is looking toward where third base would have been, taken from the approximate location of the pitcher's mound. (Photograph by the author.)

This angle is looking toward home plate from the approximate location of the pitcher's mound, looking up toward Coogan's Bluff. (Photograph by the author.)

Another Polo Grounds Towers sign can be found near where first base used to sit. (Photograph by the author.)

In the late 1960s, a plaque was placed near the approximate location of home plate and can be found today bolted to one of the apartment towers. (Photograph by the author.)

New York Giants legend Willie Mays, who spent many a season roaming the outfield at the Polo Grounds, was on hand to unveil the plaque, along with then New York City mayor John Lindsay, seen on the right. (Photograph by the author.)

The staircase (and iron fence) from where this shot was taken existed when the Polo Grounds still stood just to the right. The street in the middle of the photograph was the border between the Polo Grounds (which would have been on the right) and the Colonial Park housing project on the left (which was built in the 1940s, replacing the subway and elevated car repair shops that were there). In the center of the photograph is the old Yankee Stadium. (Photograph by the author.)

This crumbling staircase located on Coogan's Bluff leading down to where the Polo Grounds used to be is structurally all that is left of anything connected to the park. The 80-step structure was a 1913 gift to the city of New York from the owner of the baseball Giants and was later donated to the parks department by the team. Today the staircase is in disrepair and closed to the public, although there is a movement afoot to restore the staircase and landing. (Photograph by the author.)

This image is looking down at the staircase from atop Coogan's Bluff. This is bit of a dangerous climb, and it is not suggested the reader attempt it. Writer Roger Angell wrote "It's the only ballpark built against a cliff, Coogan's Bluff, so that a patron could walk downhill to a seat. You came slowly down the John T. Brush stairs to the cool of the evening, looking down at the flags and the tiers of brilliant floodlights on the stands and, beyond them, at the softer shimmer of lights on the Harlem River." It is fortuitous that stairs are still here. (Photograph by the author.)

Here is a close-up of the inlaid wording on the staircase landing. A *New York Times* article from July 9, 1913, says that on that day the baseball club would be formally presenting the "John T. Brush Stairway" to the city. The Giants' team president, H. N. Hempstead, was to present the gift to the city parks commissioner, Charles B. Stover, to honor Brush, the Giants owner who had died in 1912. (Photograph by the author.)

This view looks toward the new Yankee Stadium from atop Coogan's Bluff. (Photograph by the author.)

One hundred years ago, fans would climb these rocks to watch games at the Polo Grounds, located below at the bottom of Coogan's Bluff, in Coogan's Hollow. From this perch, they could see an obstructed view of the ball games without having to pay. (Photograph by the author.)

Here is another shot of the rocks where fans would gather with the old Yankee Stadium peeking through the Polo Grounds Towers. (Photograph by the author.)

THE SITE OF THE POLO GROUNDS TODAY

On the day the photographs in this chapter were taken, the author and his son Charlie (left) met a local named Raymond, who guided them around the former site of the Polo Grounds. At that point, he had lived in the Polo Grounds Towers for 35 years. In this shot the guys are standing at the actual site of home plate. (Photograph by the author.)

Here the author stands at the home plate plaque, which is about 20 yards away from the actual site of the base. To return to this place today is to insert oneself into one of baseball's most hallowed plots of land, a former pasture where Giants once roamed and where monumental events took place. It is sacred. And it is forever. (Photograph by Charlie Epting.)

Visit us at
arcadiapublishing.com

CPSIA information can be obtained
at www.ICGtesting.com
Printed in the USA
LVHW060559010920
664725LV00026B/1693